ADDICTED TO AN ADDICT

Letter To My Sweater

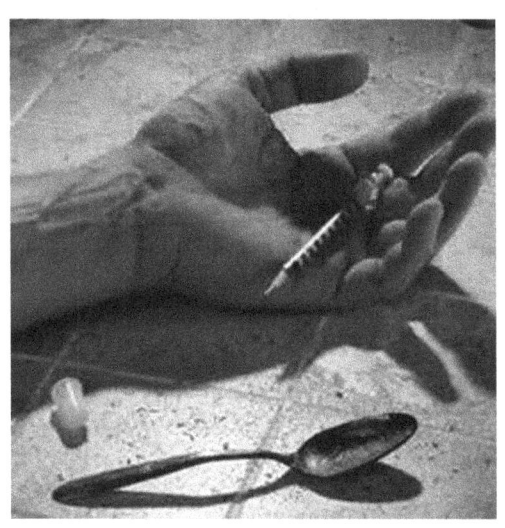

Paula Albin

Acknowledgements:

Thanks to Jeff Regan, You have been there to help me rebuild my life more than a few times.

Barbara Haines, M.A.Ed. your guidance, wisdom and suggestion to write this "letter to my sweater" made all this possible.

Mary Beth Ellis for your final edit and suggestions.

Kerrie Stephens for having a hand to hold, an ear to listen and a shoulder to cry on.

Julia my heart breaks you for and I send love and light.

My mother Susan Oliver for all her love and support.

And finally to Chuck Lesher and Writers Cramp Publishing for helping turn my nightmare into a dream come true.

All characters, places or events portrayed in this book are accurate to the best of the author's knowledge and any disagreement with this portrayal will be taken under advisement.

Publication Date: June 2014
Print ISBN 978-1-938586-69-9
eBook ISBN 978-1-938586-70-5

All Rights Reserved
Copyright © 2014 by Paula Albin

Printed in the United States of America
Writers Cramp Publishing
http://www.writerscramp.us/
editor@writerscramp.us

I grew up in Baltimore City, MD. I have called many places home since I left there: New York, New Mexico, Florida, Kuwait, and Arizona. I am a divorced mother who works in and for my community. I am not just a survivor but an overcomer of addiction. I choose not to be a statistic or a victim. I am a proud member of the Bicentennial Lion's Club, High Desert Helpers, and work at an elementary school.

"My success is not measured in money, but by the lives I touch every day and the people who love me for who I am."

Addicted to an Addict

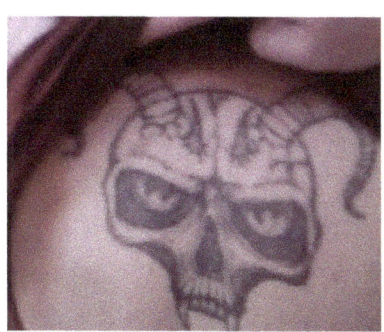

Evil tattoo on his back

Dedicated to the memory of Darrell~

May you slay your demons and find peace on your journey as I am searching for the same.

I'll see you on the other side…

∞ Paula

Addicted to an Addict

FORWARD	1
IN THE BEGINNING	2
WELCOME TO THE JUNGLE	6
THE SWEATER	10
HALL SEX	13
A LITTLE BIT OF NORMAL	17
THE OASIS IN THE DESERT	21
WELCOME TO YOUR LIFE	26
BROKEN ARM- BROKEN PROMISE	31
THE CHRISTMAS GIFT	38
LET'S CELEBRATE RECOVERY	43
PAINTED NAILS	47
PATIENCE IS A VIRTUE	50
EGGSHELLS & BOMBSHELLS	56
SICK TWIST OF FATE	65
ON THE MOVE	69
R-E-S-P-E-C-T	72
RIDE OF THE CALVARY	76
TRIALS AND TRIBULATIONS	79

Poems

A Broken Road	9
Best Wishes	12
Our Time	16
Family Tree	20
The Promise Curse	25
The Pond	30
The Pills	37
Insane Xmas	42
Fallen Angel	46
Painted Nails	49
A Gift for your Birthday	55
Cleaning Out The Closet	64
Dance with Death	68
Buried Treasure	71
Leaving Me	75
The Hero	78
She is ME	86

FORWARD

Who am I to write a book? Me...I'm nobody. I'm a Plain-Jane ordinary girl. I am the love-child of a flower-child. I guess it depends on who you ask. I'm a middle-aged, moody, mommy. I'm a pretty poet. I'm an ex-wife, taxpayer, homeowner, rescuer who stays too busy for a real relationship. When I'm not working my full time job, I am volunteering somewhere as a member of some community organization. Did I mention I was a mother? I'm also a social butterfly, hermit soul, super hero. I've also been known to a few as a Goddess. But none of these titles are who I am. These are the hats I wear or the masks I hide behind. We codependent's love our hats! We wear them proudly. I'm also a recovering addict. Not your typical alcoholic or drug addict. My drug of choice is a boy. More likely, the fantasy I carried about that boy for 27 years.

The Sweater Now

Paula Albin

IN THE BEGINNING

In The beginning God, The Universe, The Magical Stop Sign (my sister's higher power) created the World, created life and love, created boy and girl, created you and me... We are the Alpha and Omega. We are the essence of pure love and the definition of addiction. We were made for each other.

Actually we don't have to go back that far. Let's go back to 8th grade. It was a time when hair was big, music was loud and the boys were as pretty as the girls. It was a time of exploration in fashion, music and of course the opposite sex. I was a young girl coming of age.

Although I was an overachiever at school, I was lacking in social prowess. All the teachers loved me but I had few friends. I was extremely shy and grew up in a dysfunctional home. I never had the slumber parties, birthday parties or any other typical gatherings many other girls had at my age. I found any excuse not to be home to avoid listening and seeing the conflicts and abuse. I worked very hard at school to achieve praise of my teachers. At that young, tender age I would have done anything for attention. Then

Addicted to an Addict

one day I got the attention I was hopelessly yearning for.

He was a big boy. A rolly-polly looking kid with a thin smile, pretty eyes and a leather jacket. He was two years older than I was and the only kid in eighth grade with a driver's license and a car. I've seen him several times smoking in the parking lot. He was so cool and look- he smiled at me! I just blush and hide my face with my books, rushing off to class before the bell rang.

In an inner-city school with multiple classes for the same grade level, you might go an entire year without seeing the same kid twice. How it must have been fate when I see the big boy coming in late to my Social Studies class. I'm the shy girl usually sitting in the front row closest to the door with my head in a book. The quiet giant takes a seat in the back of the classroom taking a nap before lunch time. Isn't he dreamy?

Well, it's "Button Day" at the old middle school. All the most beautiful and popular girls are wearing buttons from secret and some not-so-secret admirers. All the cutest couples are posing for pictures to be placed in the yearbook sporting their shiny buttons of admiration for each other.

Paula Albin

I go to Social Studies class as usual trying not to make eye contact with all those happy giggly girls showing off their buttons and popularity. At my desk is a button of my own along with a letter. My heart is just racing. I can't believe someone left me a button! I feel so special at that moment I could cry. The letter reads; "Hey, I think you're cute. Wanna go out? Call me tonight…Wes". I was speechless. All the color must have left my face because my teacher asked if I was OK. I just nodded slowly and turned around looking that smiling boy in the face. He winked at me and my heart skipped a beat.

I met him at his house that Saturday afternoon. I told my mom I was going to church to volunteer at the soup kitchen. I volunteered often at the church. My father was already out drinking. Instead of heading to the church, I took a detour over to see Wes for our date. Wes said we were going to the movies. We were taking his car. It was a beat-up white Pinto. My own parents didn't own a car. This was all so exciting. My very first date! And what a date it would be to remember.

The roads were still icy from the late frost we had that year. I just sat back and held on tight as he maneuvered his way through traffic. Wow! I'm in a car alone with a boy who is driving. He can drive just fine but when it was time to park, he hit another car. He blamed the ice and decided we should do something else instead. We never made it to the movies that day.

Wes drove back to the neighborhood where he parked in an alley behind his house. I think he was as nervous as I was. We just sat there for what seemed to be forever. He said my pink sweater was pretty and wanted to feel how soft it was. We kissed. He felt my sweater and thank God it was a turtle neck because I was covering up a hickey for two weeks after that day. From that moment I knew he was the "One".

Paula Albin

WELCOME TO THE JUNGLE

"Welcome to my parlor said the spider to the fly..."

I hate spiders. I'm actually afraid of tarantulas. Big hairy things with 8 legs and two huge fangs that could eat your face clean off. One nice thing about living in the city is that you don't see them ever. Instead of creepy spiders crawling the streets there are things much more deadly. These are things that smile at you; things that speak pretty, sweet lies. Although these things wear clothes and walk like people, they are in fact in disguise. These things are damaged, empty souls that feed on greed, hate and fear. These things don't have a proper name so we'll just call them dealers.

Inner-city kids know the dealers. We know the poison being pushed on the streets. We know the over-all outcome and destiny of those that get trapped in the web of addiction. We've seen friends go to jail and some overdose. My friends, my family and even I have walked on the web a few times. Of course I thought that was a rite-of-passage for my age. I thought it was being "normal" to experiment. I thought it was part of the dance each child performs during those teen years. Drugs are a dance with death and I was invited to the party.

Wes and I would experiment. It was safe to try new things with the love of my life. We drank alcohol and smoked anything. He would steal his mom's pot on the regular. His father gave me my first beer. Wes's uncle taught me how to play pool at the bar. Grandma Ruth would sit in the living room and talk to me about her pet birds. What a nice family to accept me so easily and say how much they loved me. We would grow up, get married and have their grandchildren.

My mother loved Wes. She also wanted to be part of my scene. She bought us marijuana and alcohol. My mom was young and wanted acceptance too. Mom would "cover for me" when my father asked where I was. She was my friend and secretly I hated it. I hated that she was trying so hard to be cool and not be a mother. I hated that she knew what we were doing and didn't stop any of it. I hated that she paid for my poison. But in the end, I love my mother. I understand now she did the best she could with what she knew. My poor mother knew nothing about family or how to function in one. That story however is for another time.

Let's get back to the jungle. Growing up in the city is like a jungle really. Instead of trees covering the landscape we have buildings, skyscrapers and rows and rows of apartments and townhomes. Each neighborhood has an invisible boundary. In every neighborhood you have the predators that work the area. My townhome was on a corner which belonged to a dealer. Easy access for whatever medication you need.

While walking through the jungle we go in groups. It's safer that way, just like zebra or antelope. Of course, if you happen to be sent on an errand to the store alone, you go fast, don't make eye contact and don't speak to anyone. So many years I pretended to be a gazelle sprinting to the corner store and back home safely before I became the next chalk line, missing or molested. At age 14, I walked safely through those same streets with my white lion at my side. Wes was my protector, my defender and my guardian. No one would hurt me with him at my side. Besides, everyone knew him, respected him, feared him or sold him dope. I finally felt safe in my own jungle. I was a native in this land and accepted on the corner. Wes and I were wild in the streets.

A Broken Road

2011
By; Paula Oliver

On top a snow covered hill two souls melt into one
The warmth of their love Compared to the sun
On two separate paths For 23 years
Each learning lessons Full of sorrow and tears
A twist of fate Paths cross again
But only briefly Before it will end
A fork in the road They'll each say goodbye
He'll turn to leave Leave her to cry
And wonder…why?

Why Oh why this wicked road
Twist and turns While I carry the load
The heavy pieces of my shattered soul
My broken heart will never be whole…

THE SWEATER

It was late November and there was a chill in the air. We were doing what we always did; sitting on a snow-covered hill looking out over the harbor. We would do that for hours. I would lean into him for warmth and to be close. Wes would wrap his arms around me and tell me he would always keep me safe. That day I was complaining about the weather and how we should just go home. He looked me in the eyes saying how he loved me and would give me the world. I responded with "I don't want the world; only the clothes off your back" and at that point he removed that ugly gray sweater he got from his grandma. I couldn't find the words... I just hugged him hard and kissed him slowly all the while thinking...yeah this is the "One".

After that day, we were always together. We went to and from school together. I studied and he would just sit with me while I did homework. Wes and I were thicker than thieves. There was never a day we were apart. I even dragged him to church once in awhile. Sometimes Wes would talk me into skipping school and playing video games

The Sweater Then

all day. He would have friends bring beer and drugs and we partied all day. I would have the house empty and cleaned before my father came home from work. What an adventure we were having! I was partying like my parents did on the weekends.

Somehow I managed to keep my grades passing enough to start high school. Wes was not so fortunate. Right before summer break, he was escorted out of the building in handcuffs on charges of distribution of a controlled substance. I knew that principal didn't like him, but really? He gave me an aspirin when I said I had a headache. Everyone knew he was dealing something but for him to be expelled for aspirin was wrong. And more importantly, it was my fault. I cried and screamed for them to let him go. I tried so hard to save him from this injustice. Instead of Wes turning to me for support, he dumped me. That bastard! He promised me the World.

Best Wishes

BY: Paula Oliver
1987
RE: Happy New Year

Seasons greetings and happy New Year,
To someone I thought was very dear.
Seasons have changed and so have you,
In all good time things will renew.
I'm wishing you good will and yuletide,
So let's put all bad feelings aside?
Going toward the year 1988,
We look back on our past mistakes.
Now you know how it feels to be free,
But the only true love you had was me.
You were my first but not my last,
Next time I won't move so fast.
Since our romance had to end,
Let's take a chance and be friends.
Even if things aren't the same,
Let's have our friendship still remain…

HALL SEX

I didn't take rejection well. I guess nobody really does. I was going to make him pay for dumping me. I started dating his friends. I made sure to go to every party he would be at. I wanted him to see me with the latest boy toy. I wanted to make him jealous. I wasn't going to let him forget me. Wes couldn't forget me anyway. I was his first love as he was mine. We would be drinking and smoking and hanging out at these parties. I would pass him in the hall and he would say "Fuck you" and I would reply "never again!" This would go on for 3 years. Sometimes we would be so drunk we would kiss in the halls instead of screaming at each other. Other times you could see graffiti we would write about each other we left for one another. The love-hate war was on. All this time, he didn't even date another girl. He was a drunk, drugged-up drop out. Who would want him? Maybe me...

It's a typical Saturday night in the city. The usual stupid parties are happening. I stop by the regular houses to get a drink or get high before roaming the streets. I don't see Wes anywhere. I was drinking pretty heavy and was asking about him too much. A mutual friend of ours said Wes was at another house party. He walked me to the other party. I was looking for Wes hoping to either make-out or fight with the love of my life. I heard his voice in the crowd coming from the kitchen. I wished I never walked in. I see him and he sees me. He started screaming *"Get her out of here now!"* but it's too late. I seen the needle in his arm. Everything else fades to black. I fainted. I actually fainted for the first time in my life.

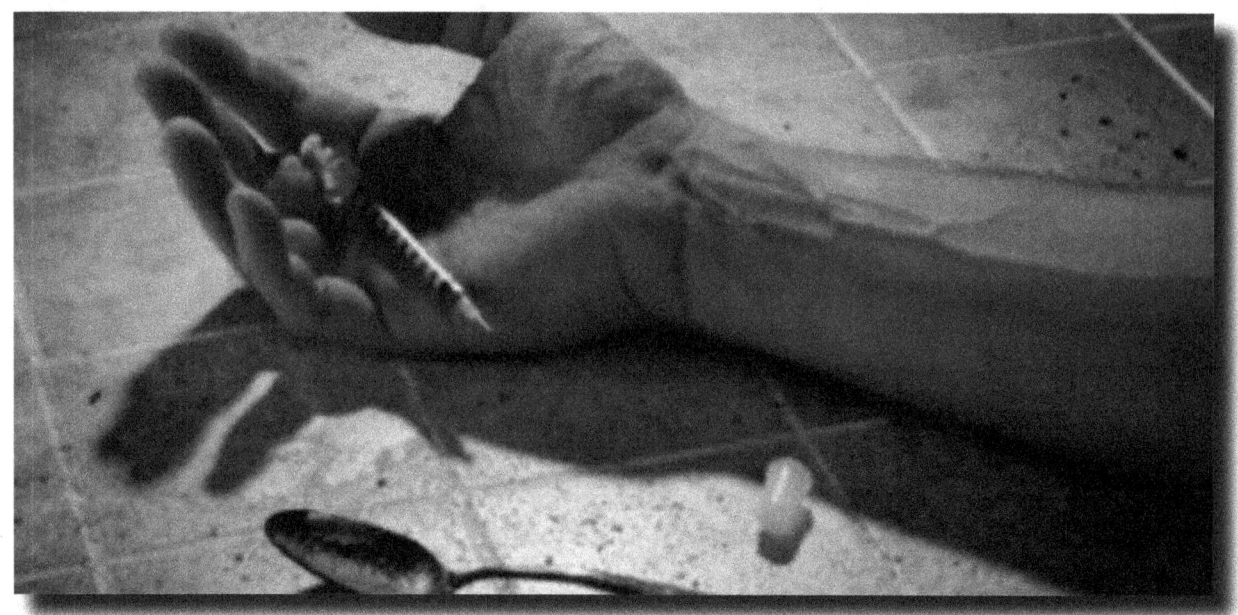

 I left...everything. I left school, I left the city, I left home. I left with only one suitcase filled with childhood memories. I left with a sweater, a yearbook and a few pictures. And I ran away... I went to the country to stay with a cousin for a few months. I lived in an attic and just cried. I didn't drink, I didn't get high, I just sat there thinking how could I save him? What can I do? When will this nightmare be over?

Three months later I returned to the city. My parents abandoned the house and filed for divorce. My home was now a legitimate street corner ghetto crack house. No water or electric but plenty of bodies passed out around my furniture. My little sister was in rehab and was a ward of the state. I was afraid to stay in my home. I started sofa-surfing. I slept at friends' homes all the while asking about Wes. His cousin Lynda told me he ran off and got married. How could he? There was absolutely nothing left for me anymore. I wanted to die. Better yet; I would start all over again somewhere else with someone else. I left the city with the first man I could. He looked a lot like Wes. That man was heading west.

Our Time

By: Paula Oliver

When you chose to make your time with her (Heroin)
You lost your time with me
Now we live with these choices
And what will never be
I'll pack away the pictures
Events frozen in time
Of happier moments
When I was yours and you were mine
And in this box of trinkets
I'll pack away my heart
Goodbye sweater, letters, roses
Time to make a new start
You can't go back in time
To fix what has been broken
The trust, the love, the vows
Words that were never spoken
Our time now is over
Time to work, time to sleep, time to cry
Time to finally set you free
Time to say goodbye

Addicted to an Addict

A LITTLE BIT OF NORMAL

I followed Ben across the country. I followed that man across the globe. We blew into Arizona like a tumble weed. We had a great adventure planned and when he was finished tech school I would be able to go to school too. We would have had some great adventures- if only he wasn't an addict. He was addicted to the "chase" and the "need for speed". If he wasn't dreaming of racing motorcycles he was in hot pursuit of the ladies. Of course, I was very young and had no clue. I only knew I wanted to help him stop hurting me.

Ben finished school. He took another lover. Ben and I moved to another state. He started a business, slept with my best friend, we moved again. He worked for a motorcycle shop, he took two lovers and I moved away. He called me and asked me to marry him. We married, he cheated and we left yet another state. We buried our first born son, he found comfort in a coworker and we moved across the world. I guess we were running out of states in this country? You see, after so many times of moving I was tired of packing my old suitcase filled with memories and a sweater. I just had my last child. I finally found my dream house, the perfect job and I wasn't leaving anymore. I came back to the town where I buried my boy and I wasn't going to give up my life again because he wasn't able to control himself. Changing zip codes just didn't work. The problem was not the location, but the person. I changed everything about my appearance. I changed my religion. I changed my attitude. I couldn't change anymore. He still sought the company of other women.

    We sat down at the kitchen table when he came home from work. I held his hands in mine and looked into his eyes saying, "I love you enough to let you go and I love myself enough to let you go." While he was away on business I found three cell phone numbers added to our bill to three different lady friends in three separate states. I just couldn't do this adventure anymore. "I would rather be alone than lonely," and with that so ended 17 years and a one-sided marriage.

    Well so much for the white picket fence dream. I grew some in the years we were together. I started reading. I started writing. I started loving myself. I knew that when

I left the big city I was running away from my childhood. I knew that I wanted something "normal" for my life. I wanted the All American Dream. My life was going to be what I wanted and I knew I didn't want to be the "stand by" wife at home while Ben had lovers in every port. I did find it ironic that the one place I refused to leave was filled with tarantulas. I guess fate has me facing my foolish fears after all these years.

Family Tree

By: Paula Oliver

Well, I guess the rotten apple,
Doesn't fall far from the tree.
What he did to your mother,
You've now done to me…
Whether it was 40 years or 4,
It's the life I wanted to live;
But your family men need more,
Then what an honest woman can give…
Was it in the pursuit?
Having a new girl day after day?
Now you're the new recruit,
Once your father passed away…
You're the monster that you hated,
Your reflection shows your father.
How long have I waited?
Should I have even bothered?

THE OASIS IN THE DESERT

I may not have the white picket fence yet but I do own a corner lot in a beautiful little town. I do have the perfect job that fulfills my calling and pays enough for my bills. I do have a couple children that I love more than anything else. I have a great reputation and am involved in many community organizations. I love my life but feel lonely sometimes. My husband was hardly home because of his career and I was physically alone for years. I never noticed his absence. He called almost every day and stopped in to do laundry when he was in Arizona. I raised children, worked, paid bills and maintained the home while he was in pursuit of fame, fortune and lust. This arrangement worked for him for years and it would still have worked if only I would have played along. I deserve better and we co-parent nicely today. He still calls often and stops by to visit the children. The only difference is I don't have to sleep with him or wash his dirty clothes.

During the transition from filing for divorce to the actual ending of that legal contract was a difficult time. Although we agreed on most everything there was a feeling of loss. A depression and shock we all go through when someone leaves our life. Ben didn't leave my life but just changed the title and role he plays in it. The divorce was not actually an end of something as it was more a change in titles. We both are much happier today now that we can raise and share our children without hurting each other. Of all the relationships I have had in my life, the one I share with Ben is the most mature one. I wish I could say the same with the other relationships I have had.

When Ben left for good I was afraid. Afraid of being alone, not being able to make it on my own, but mostly I was afraid of losing that title "wife". I have always been something to someone and now I was losing even my title. I couldn't save him from himself. Today I know most people don't want to be saved anyway. And so as a creature who loves symbolism, I cut my wedding ring and shaped it into a broken heart, embed it into a concrete plague and hung it on my wall.

So here I am now swimming alone in my pond. I stay pretty busy but the loneliness comes creeping in the dead of the night. When the day is done, the sun is set and the house is quiet, my mind starts to wonder. I find myself

Addicted to an Addict

playing the "what if" game in my head. And finally after many sleepless hours I go find a distraction. I want to stop thinking so I sit myself in front of a computer and play games. Mindless chatter on social networks along with a few rounds of bingo and I should be able to sleep. My "what ifs" start turning to "what ever happened to" and soon I am surfing head first on the internet.

It wasn't hard to find Wesley. It seems that he likes the social networks too. No picture in place but the name and the city are a match. I'll drop an email and see what happens. The next day I get a response. It's not who I thought it was but close to it. It's the old man senior. How fantastic! We start communicating daily about my life and about his son. How fate has brought me exactly what I asked for. I hear Wes is divorced and is getting released from prison soon. He has no children and no where to go when he gets out. Dad asked if Wes could write me sometime. Of course he can! I'm so lonely and would love to hear from him again. It's been 23 years and I live 2300 miles away so we have a lot of ground to cover.

I receive a belated birthday card in the mail postmarked from a Maryland Correctional Facility. The letter that accompanied the card was full of metaphors, poetry and spelling errors. The slanted print was the same as the letters I had in my old worn suitcase. I was delighted. All the selected happy memories came rushing back. My first true love was reaching out to me. He never stopped thinking about me. Wes was still in love with the memory of our yesterday and he wanted me back. Of course when you've been in the system for 11 years, it's just a thing they call "jail talk". I didn't know. How could I? I've chosen a different path to walk my life on. Nonetheless, I was no longer a sensible adult but a love-struck teen reaching out to a long-lost love fated to be mine. I would finally be able to save him from life, bad choices and destruction.

Throughout the correspondence between us, Wes promised not to make a "ripple in my pond" but just wanted a normal life. He wanted respect without fear. Wes wanted a family who loved and supported him. Mostly he wanted to live a clean life without drugs. As a divorcee with two young children and a great reputation in my community, I could give him everything he wanted. Without delay Wes landed in Arizona. This begins our great dysfunctional adventure of love, hate and addiction.

The Promise Curse

2011
By; Paula Oliver

I'll cast away this demon I'll break free from your spell
I'll throw a curse upon you And send you back to hell
With every once of energy I pray with all my might
Every time you close your eyes I haunt your every night
May fate give you your just dessert
No more pleasure only hurt
With each one of my angry tears
May life add to your many years
To suffer in pain and doubt
May you always go without
May you know no love or friend
Even to your very end
When death comes with sweet release
Even then find no peace
For this one thing you promised me
Your heart and soul for eternity

Paula Albin

WELCOME TO YOUR LIFE

The first year was amazing. I was drunk for much of it. During my adult life I did not drink or do drugs. I was playing the perfect wife, mother, worker person. I didn't do anything I thought would be wrong or dysfunctional. I was rebelling against my childhood by being the white sheep of a black sheep family. I aspired to be "Donna Reed" or "Mrs. Cleaver". I was as normal as I could be. Then you came back. You wanted to celebrate. We went to the local bar; which I usually didn't do, and we shot pool, drank beer and talked with the locals. You looked around and said "this is our kind of people". That night you shared terrible secrets. You told me things I will never repeat. I shared heartaches and headaches. You cried and I cried and then we fell asleep in each other's arms.

I called you "my great distraction" which you hated. I knew I was lonely and didn't want to grieve over my divorce anymore. I wanted to be lost in you. I wanted a title, a purpose, but mostly I wanted to believe in fate and true love. Loves conquers all! Love saves me and love saves you. The sad truth is love doesn't cure addiction. I could never have loved you enough to save you. I could barely save myself from you in the end.

When you arrived you had nothing. But you wrote me letters daily and left them for me on mirrors, in drawers and in text. I bought you a phone, clothes, a truck and opened my home to you. My children were in awe with your tattoos and tough exterior. They were lonely too. We were going to play house and see how it goes. I introduced you to my friends and around town. I pulled some strings to get you a job. With a vehicle and employment with benefits you were on your way to the normal life.

I got sick. How fate has twisted yet again. I was coughing bright red blood and was afraid. I was dying and you were there. You left work and met me at the hospital. You didn't want to lose me again. The doctors were baffled. They mumbled something about Cancer and sent me home with a brochure to die. That night it happened again and I was rushed back to the emergency room. You never left my side. Once again I was sent home with the explanation that the hospital was not equipped to help me and I needed to follow up with a specialist. You quit your job to stay with me and within three months we had seen that specialist. There was nothing wrong after all. Something must have torn somewhere in my lung but no cancer was detected. You asked me to marry you. You wanted me forever and didn't ever want to live without me. I was overjoyed with the prospect of a long, healthy life with my love. We stopped drinking. I never liked drinking anyway. We could have just as much fun sober. Besides we are living a clean life like you said you wanted. And so our story continues. You are now unemployed but emotionally supporting me the whole way through the storm. In my closet hangs that gray ugly sweater you gave me 23 years ago. It still fits me nicely and I wear it often.

You wanted to start your own business. I bought you business cards, uniforms and started promoting you to the town. You were on your way to your new life. There was nothing you couldn't have. The respect and good reputation you wanted was all here. You had an instant family, a new business and a good woman supporting you. You also needed a new truck. This old white truck didn't have character. No worries. You'll start making money soon and we'll make it. The house wasn't to your liking and slowly you started replacing everything in it. I didn't mind. You told me once "everything is replaceable" and I tried to understand how you wanted to make it your

place too. It's ok. We'll get another refrigerator, stove, bed, furniture, etc. We painted all the rooms a different color. I even bought a pool table for you so you wouldn't be tempted to go to the bar. I also bought you a trailer for a quiet space whenever you wanted to escape the house. Whatever made you happy because you made me happy. We would be happy together!

The Pond

2014
By: Paula Oliver

Once upon a time in the deep blue sea

There were two young fish one you one was me.

We swam in the reef we swam in school

We were young we were foolish

We were guppies being cool

But the tides that churn and wind that blew

Flooded the sea sweeping me from you

Over time I have guppies of my own

You still swimming alone with no home

You promised me no ripples in my pond

All the while I was being conned

You didn't grow into a guppy like me

But a piranha mean and deadly…

BROKEN ARM- BROKEN PROMISE

    The 2nd year brought us many challenges. While working hard in the Arizona summer sun you tripped with a refrigerator and broke your arm. You were rushed to the hospital and I was by your side. I couldn't believe you were injured. What was I to do? You work so hard for so very little moving furniture, cutting grass, building structures. It seems like you never have money and all you have to show for it now is a broken arm. "Darrell'll Do It" was printed on those business cards and you sure did it this time!

    The nurses tell me you were combative and did not want sedation. When you woke up with a Morphine drip, you ripped it out of your arm. You explained to the doctors that you were a recovered heroin addict and did not want narcotics of any sort. I was so proud of you. However, you did reluctantly fill that prescription of pain killers in case that arm started hurting. You also said your back always hurt. Something to take the edge off is ok. As long as you are responsible with your medication you won't fall back into the grips of addiction. I'll be right here watching over you. We'll get through this.

The arm- it hurts all the time. The medication doesn't work. You say the metal they put in there is rubbing and so we have it removed. I made a wind chime out of it. Just another piece of you I have to add to my collection. The sweater, the pictures, the letters and now the chimes.

This accident left us reconsidering your career options. There is no reason you should have to work so hard. You are going to school. You old man was an A/C tech and so you shall be. I can support the house while you continue your education. When you graduate you will be working and making good money. Then we can have that wedding we have been talking about. We've been putting spare change in a jar now for over a year. It seems that the money jar is always half empty? Speaking of your father, it seems that he is restless and wants to move out here to be close to family. This is great! I have plenty of room for him here. Since you are between jobs and your school is out over the summer it's the perfect time to move your dad out from the east coast. One big happy family!

Once dad moved in it seemed that you were still lonely and distant. I know I work a lot and volunteer many hours in the community but I try to make time for you too. I also give you the space you need. I know you don't like my friends so I spend less and less time with any of them. My social time is spent with you. You contact a few friends on the east coast and this summer they are coming to visit. How nice, more house guests. I usually don't have company and hosting your friends sounds like fun. It's only for a few weeks. I'm sure to make a good impression and they'll like me. You said they were your best friends and you needed their approval of me if we were to be married. No pressure there, right?

You best friend Tom is quiet and you tell me that you guys did some time together in jail. He's hard to talk to. We really have nothing in common besides you. His wife Angie is pretty. She's a chatterbox with not much substance to bring to a conversation. She also seems to be against wearing clothing suited for her age or size. It is summer time and they are company so I put on a happy face and make nice. They like spending time alone with you and seem uneasy in my company. I am glad when the visit is over. I feel like I missed something but lately many things have gone missing. Maybe I need a vacation from all this vacationing. Glad I have work to do.

Angie must have enjoyed the visit because she sent you a package in the mail after they arrived home. You left the package in the car. I opened it to find pills. What the hell is Suboxin? Of course you don't stick around to tell me. You and your father move out after that argument. Your father tells me he thinks you are on the dope again and he's leaving. He says you are sick and he doesn't want you stealing from him. He's going back east.

You are sick! You have been throwing up and can't hold anything down. You tell me it's your liver and you need help. You refuse to go see the doctor but ask for money for medicine. I reluctantly give you money. I also buy you liquid meal supplements hoping that will put some weight on you. You are still going to school and I see you often when you call for money or food or company. You finally have the courage to tell me the Suboxin is medicine for addicts. Angie is an addict. I can only assume that Tom must be too. You tell me you need it to stay straight and you are trying real hard to do so. You made a mistake when they came to visit and you were sorry. Your father left you on your own and you had no way of paying your bills or making your own way. I was so worried! Thank God the landlord was a friend of mine and she let you stay as long as you did for free. Of course you can come home and I will help you. That's what love is all about, right?

Coming home sick is better than not coming home at all. You are just too sick to work but at least you go to night school. I don't mind sharing the car. I guess you had to sell the trucks for living expenses. While you were living across town you made some new friends too. Biker Mike stopped by saying you owed him $40.00. I paid him right away without asking questions. It happens. I always have enough to help you. Also seen dirty Val. You know the girl I told you I didn't like. She's got a real bad reputation in this town. She stopped by to see if you were around. Yet again another fight. You explain to me that she had some pain pills for you because the doctor won't write you any more prescriptions and your arm really hurts. You also tell me that you are not a cheater and you are not my ex-husband. You would never do anything like that to disrespect or dishonor me.

Of course you hurt. Your life is full of pain and bad choices. You say to me "I love you honey, gimme $20" and

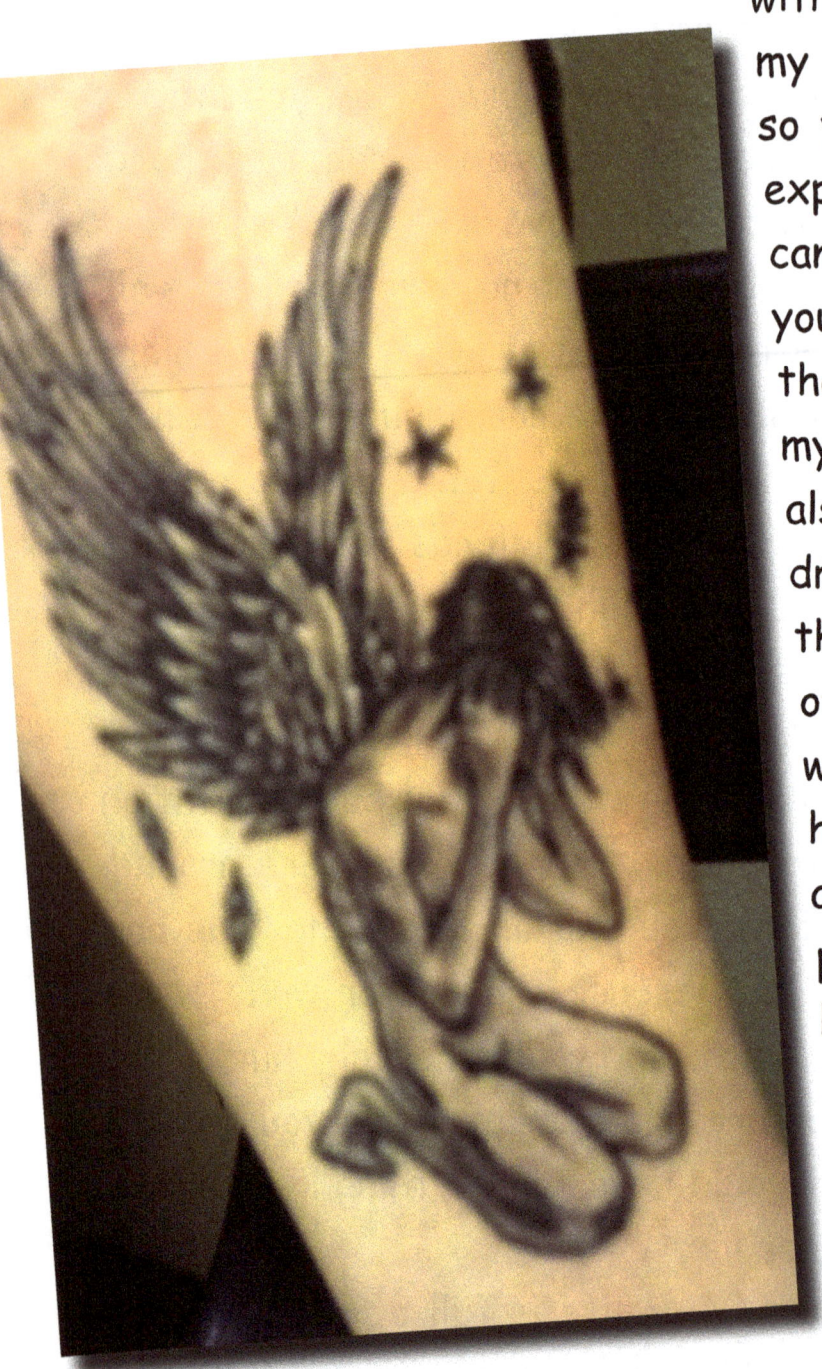

with that I hand you my last bit of money so you feel better. I explain to you that I cannot afford to buy you pills every day and that these are "not my kind of people". I also explain that the drama has to stop at the gate and no more of your friends are welcome here. I do have a reputation and children to protect from this kind of lifestyle. It is supposed to be you and me. Tell the rest of them to stay away.

The Pills

9/3/11
BY: Paula Oliver

The pills the pills Your wicked addiction
The cause of my pain And my heart condition
Once it was good Filled with love and hope
Now it is broken Because of your dope
My was love was eternal My love was strong
But you chose poorly you chose wrong
So pack your bags Leave my home
To the streets where you can roam
To chase those pills that keep you numb
One day realize that you were dumb
To choose the pills over me
Who would have loved you for eternity…

Paula Albin

THE CHRISTMAS GIFT

It's that time of year again. Carolers singing, lights strung on the cactus and shiny presents under the tree. I gave you money to buy me a Valentine's present two months ago. I heard later you also borrowed $40.00 from a mutual friend of ours to buy me a present. The flowers and candy were nice but I am sure it wasn't $60.00. You didn't even ask me this time for money to buy me something for Christmas. Your mom sent you $2000 and I guess that I will finally get that ring you have been promising me. You also cashed a student loan check from school. It looks like it is going to be a great Christmas.

The children are away with their father and it is just you and me for two weeks. Your school is on holiday break and I'm off work too. You've been sick again and I am guessing it's your liver. Poor guy seems to be sick a lot lately. Even being sick you still manage to smile; or sleep. You sleep for hours-sometime days. I hope for a quick recovery so we can spend some time together.

You feel well enough to go shopping. You bought yourself some jewelry. I call it bling. A grown man wearing a gold chain necklace and bracelet is so ghetto. I know if you are buying such nice jewelry for yourself then you are probably buying something really nice for me. If you did buy me anything I never did get it.

While having one of your many bouts with vomiting you come to me saying you need to go to the doctor. I was worried as I usually am when you get so sick. You need some cash and I offer to drive you. You said no that you would be back shortly but needed some cash to be seen. I protest but think maybe I'll clean the house and make some dinner while you are at urgent care.

Well, it has been hours since you left. Dinner is cold and I have been calling every hospital in the city. I've called every urgent care also. I have to wait 24 hours before I can call the police. I'm so worried that you are laying dead somewhere. You don't answer the cell phone and I can't imagine what ever happened? I could call and report the car stolen but I did let you borrow it. I blow out the candles and just wait by the door. Yet another lonely night without you.

You return but the car has been damaged. The whole front and side panels are destroyed. The story you give doesn't make any sense. You talk something about a motorcycle cutting you off on the highway and you riding the guardrail. You said the police were there but didn't catch the guy. There is no police report and I can't get a straight story about where it all happened. When I mention contacting the insurance company you tell me to drop it. You would have it fixed yourself. Your jewelry was also missing. You said you must have left it at the doctor's office but could not remember which office that was. I finally had to sell the car for scrap metal after two years of waiting for you to get it fixed.

    It is Christmas Eve and you have to go to the airport to pick up a friend. I guess I'll do some laundry and make dinner so we have clean socks and a nice meal when you return. I'll put something pretty one. I know you love me in white. I have just the outfit. Then it happened…

    I found your needle in the hallway on the floor. I just stood there for a minute. My head starts to spin and all I see is red right before everything goes black. I can't believe you dropped it. I can't believe you have been lying for so very long. I can't believe my entire body, my heart and my soul shut down and I fainted.

Addicted to an Addict

When you finally returned home I was waiting by the door. I went through your things. I searched your textbooks, your clothes, your shelves. I didn't find anything else. But here I held a needle in my hand. It was physical proof that you are dirty. I yelled, I cried, and finally I packed your bags for you. I told you to go...again. I also told you to call me when you're sober. I said I love you and I know we'll be together again one day. You left for the big city on January 8th at 3pm. I cried again.

Insane Xmas

BY: Paula Oliver

Seething hatred pierce my brain, My icy skin crawls.
Doctors say that I'm insane, Trapped behind these walls...
Darkness has engulfed me, No one hears my screams.
All I have is memory, Or were they only dreams?...
How long has it been? Since I had a family.
I can't remember when, When I lost all reality...
Christmas around the corner, Death – a welcomed gift!
Without friend or mourner, My spirits set adrift...
Alas, poor Santa's passed me by, Forced to live another year.
Try to hold back the cries, Wipe away the tears...

LET'S CELEBRATE RECOVERY

All I can do is cry and write. I keep a journal since the day you left. I barely function at work and I am no kind of mother. I have almost completely shut down. Then a friend of mine invited me to a meeting. She said it might help to talk about it. I was ready to try anything to stop crying. I couldn't look at myself anymore in the mirror. The meeting was on Friday.

My friend Michelle picked me up at home and she drove me to the meeting. It was a church based self help group filled with all kinds of dysfunctional addictions and problems. I was barely aware what was unfolding around me. I must have looked like I wasn't happy since no one would talk to me. I didn't care. I was still numb and going through the motions. The meeting had a message; one I didn't even hear, and some singing. They passed a plate where I dropped a dollar in and then it was time for groups.

This seemed to me like any other church service. I've been to many as a child and it didn't touch my heart or open my soul. I would have left early if I drove myself. It was a girl-only session and soon the group was going around the circle each sharing why they were there. There were a few alcoholics, more than a few co-dependants, and then there she was. She was the leader of the meeting. Nan was a tall, older woman with beautiful long blonde hair. She was a recovering Heroin addict. She was glorious with her words and kindness. I was awestruck. I wanted so much to reach out to her. She beat this damn disease. She understood how Wes was feeling and the road he was on. I wanted to be her best friend. Nan had the answers I've been searching for. She could help me help save Wesley.

When the time came for me to share I cried. I poured my heart out onto the table and told those strangers everything about my lost love and the needle. I even talked a minute about my ex-husband and the 17 years I shared with him. Everyone was crying and nodding. They understood my pain and Nan knew all too well the struggle for sobriety. I felt a great weight lift off my shoulders. There was healing in sharing. But more importantly there were answers and information. The more I could learn from Nan and her group the better prepared I can be when Wes needs me to help. I will be able to finally save him.

When I left that night I took every brochure and number I could carry. I took the handouts, I left all my contact information and I signed up for the newsletter and email. I was arming myself for the greatest battle I would ever face. I needed an arsenal and a mini army if I would be fighting for my love.

I attended every Friday night meeting I could. I was so overjoyed when the meetings moved to my town. They would be every Friday night right across the street from my house. It just couldn't be easier. I also started attending the local AA groups and was looking to starting an NA group for all these lost locals who needed rescuing. When the meetings didn't seem to be enough I would meet with a few women from the group at the park or coffee shop to talk about addictions. I was going to save the whole town from addiction. So when Wesley did finally return to me clean and sober there would be no one left in this town to tempt him. Did I mention I am a superhero?

Paula Albin

Fallen Angel
By: Paula Oliver

Like an angel fallen from grace,
You lay broken on the floor.
Living with your shame and disgrace,
Remembering how it was before…
Your wings have been bruised,
Your halo has lost its shine.
You feel dirty and used,
Thinking of what you left behind…
You wondered out of the "garden",
Looking for a new paradise.
Left my heart to harden,
Left my soul to sacrifice…
Come back to the light,
I'll lift you up – help you rise.
We'll make it all wrongs right,
We'll say no more "goodbyes"…

Addicted to an Addict

PAINTED NAILS

It has been 4 months since you left my little town to go to the city. You called me on Valentine's Day to ask for money. You said you kind of missed me and was wondering if I was seeing anyone yet. That's such a crazy question. All I have been doing every night is crying, praying, writing and lighting a candle for you. I hardly sleep and when I do I only dream of you. I'm so glad to hear you are still going to school and that you are clean. You refused to admit the needle was ever yours. Maybe the dog is using drugs now? I open the box to check sometimes to see if the needle is still there. If only it wasn't there I could tell myself I just made it all up. I would rather be crazy than admit you are an active addict. I'd rather loose my sanity than my heart.

I've been reading too. I read about addiction, about love and poetry. I go to meetings and I paint my nails. I painted them all black. Every month you are away from me I paint them black except for one. I add a new nail to the colors every month you are gone. When the 10 nails are colored again it would be 10 months since you've been gone. I believe you will be clean by then or gone forever. I believe that if I just wait it out and keep praying you will return. I have the same dream every night. You knock on my door and when I answer, you have flowers and a ring. You are on one knee and ask me proper to marry you.

Since you left I sleep with your sweater. I write to you in my journal. I write you poetry. And of course I cry myself to sleep, wrapped in your blanket and think about dying. I dream I am drowning or suffocating. These emotions are endless and I can't continue with the pain. I tried to drink myself to death only to have a horrible hangover the next day. When I get to death thinking I usually pull myself out of it knowing that this is temporary and you will return. You will keep your promises and be the man I want you to be. You will accept me and love me knowing I have been a faithful good woman waiting for you.

I paid the local handyman Bill to take the pieces of iron you left to finish the gazebo you never really started. We could be married right there! I planted a poppy field in your honor. As usual I am the creature of symbolism. I planted roses also. I painted everything black. I made candles and sold my soul to the most powerful to bring you home. There is nothing I would not do to have you back. There is nothing I would not give. I wait by the phone, by the door, by candlelight. I wait.

Addicted to an Addict

Painted Nails

9/11/11
BY: Paula Oliver

10 fingernails I paint black,
and once a month I take one back.
10 months will have come and gone,
That's plenty of time for me to move on.
By then it will all seem,
Nothing more than a distant dream.
Maybe I shall paint them yellow,
To attract a new young fellow?
Or purple, orange, an array of blues,
There are so many I could choose!
Pink, green or red like my heart,
I'm not sure just where to start.
But not yet- I need time to heal,
There is still so much sadness left to feel.
Maybe faith, hope and love will bring you back,
Buy not today- my nails are painted black…

PATIENCE IS A VIRTUE

    I guess all good things do come to those who wait. I have been so diligent with my vigil to my long lost love. And then you called. You sounded desperate. You needed me to help you. You said my love would save you. You just got out of detox. You needed to go through rehab and was looking to stay at a local halfway house in the city. You had taken a leave of absence from school and hit bottom. I was so shocked to hear your voice. I called my best friend Connie and asked her to stay with my children while I drove to the city to rescue you.

    I looked up a halfway house you could stay at. I paid for it online and got the directions. I found you in the downtown area. You looked more dead than alive. You were too thin and old looking. You were dirty and hungry. What did you do to yourself? How could I have let this happen? How did I fail you? What could I do to make you better now?

    Before we ever made it to the halfway house I drove through a fast food restaurant. I bought you something

Addicted to an Addict

to eat and a soda. We drove around and you just sat there. We went shopping at a dollar store for anything you might need or want. You must have been exhausted from the months you've spent on the streets. I was here now and I was going to make it all better. My love would conquer all. Off to the treatment center and your recovery.

The place was miserable. It was dirty and scary and I didn't feel at all safe. But they had a bed for you and

a program. It wasn't cheap by my standards but it sure wasn't very welcoming either. All the things I bought for you (clothes, soap, etc.) had to be stored for 3 days. The bedbugs were a problem. You got a cot and a room to share with 3 other men. Is this what prison is like without the fence? I just held you in my arms for a minute and then I had to let you go. I cried the two hour drive home.

That night I told the children you were ok but you were sick. I explained that you would be coming home one day when you were all better. We would be a family again soon. You had to go to the hospital and get better first. We started making plans for your return home. Then we slept. I slept dreamless and solid for the first time in months. I was going to have the life I wanted with the man I wanted in my life. This was just a detour to the goal at the end.

You called me at work from the program. You explained that you were going to 90 meetings in 90 days. It would be a 3 month program and then you could come home. I was so excited! The children and I made plans to see you every weekend. We packed a picnic lunch and headed to the big city to spend the day with you. All of us went to your weekend meetings. The meetings always seem to be in the worst part of the city. During one of the meetings I thought to myself "these are not my kind of people" which I regretted thinking. I was not one to pass judgment but honestly I didn't think the kids should be hearing these awful things. This is exactly what I ran away from as a child. While I am saving you from this disease who is saving the kids from the effects of this disease?

After several long hot rides with 2 screaming kids to the city I decided that it was best to no longer take the weekend trips. I got you a cell phone and bought you everything you needed. I even sent you money when you called and asked. I would wait here and continue working while you continued treatment. Its only 2 hours downtown and then 2 hours return but I just don't have the time to work a full day and cook, clean, homework, bath and get ready to do it again. I know you are disappointed but I am sure you understand I have to maintain the house while you are away.

I do make trips to see you but no longer bring the children. This dysfunction is not for them to understand. They should not have to suffer through this. Since the weekend visits have stopped, you want to leave early. Of course if you say you are cured then I will be there to bring you home. You know better than anyone else that you are really ready to start living a clean life. I believe you and believe in you. You sneak out of the place in the middle of the night. It doesn't feel right to leave like that but you say the place is too dirty and the people there are active addicts. It's a risk to your sobriety to stay. Besides we have meetings across the street and two at the library. We can finish cleaning up from home.

Too bad once you came home the meetings stopped. I understand you couldn't find a sponsor you liked and you say no one really understands your unique problem. I looked at all the meetings and found several people who would have sponsored you but you decline. You said it will work best if I just keep reminding you to be clean. Now that I know what dirty looks like I can stop it before it happens. You officially hand over your sobriety to me to control. That's the perfect gift for a codependent to have. Thank you for feeding my addiction by handing me yours. So I watch and I wait for any sign you might be slipping.

Addicted to an Addict

A Gift for your Birthday
9/29/13
By: Paula Oliver

I bought you a gift but it won't do,
So this year I'm giving you something new...
Freedom!
You are free- I release you and your energy.
You are free to be who you want to be.
Free to love or free to hate
Free to work or procrastinate
Free to listen or free to talk
Free to rest or free to walk
Free to fight or free to play
I give you more freedom each day
Free to climb and free to stumble
Free to be proud free to be humble
Free to learn and free to teach
I give you your freedom of speech
Free to act and free to think
Free to swim or free to sink
You are now free to feel
Free to hurt and free to heal
Free to fly or free to fall
Free to lay down or stand tall
Free to truth or free to lie
Free to smile and free to cry
Know I loved you to the end
You've always had free choice my friend-
Happy birthday

EGGSHELLS & BOMBSHELLS

The relationship has changed and now instead of being an adult in my home you become a dependant in every sense of the word. You have burned many bridges the last time you were here. You owe most of the addicts in town. We laugh at them because who are they going to call? What are they going to do? Now that you are clean you don't need to know them anymore.

Of course you also burned a few good people in this town too. Work is slow at best since you left so many unfinished projects all around town. Many people just don't want you working in their homes. Even with my recommendations and great reputation it is hard to find work for you. That's ok. More time at home means more self improvement. Besides I could use some help maintaining the house and raising the children. I'm glad you are home and we are a family again.

That leave of absence for your school has run out. I know you are disappointed that you can't get to school but you already had 3 vehicles. I am left with only 1 and I need to get to work. Besides you have acquired some knowledge and can still work somewhere. I introduce you to Billy the local handyman.

Before long you and Billy are great friends. Billy gives you a lot of work and you are making some money for yourself. You hardly ever ask me for money. I already established that I will not hand you money but will buy you whatever you ask if I can. Part of keeping you sober means handling your expenses without enabling you to have extra money to buy dope. More and more this feels like I am baby-sitting rather than sharing a life with an equal partner.

You don't like working for Billy. You don't like working for anyone but yourself really. I understand it is hard to do what other people say and you like to be in charge but that is something you work toward. I read somewhere that delayed gratification is difficult for addicts. I point out all the projects you left here at the house you can finish but they hold no meaning for you now. They just sit there. The junk pile in the backyard is reaching dangerous levels and it would be nice if that was cleaned. I find more and more of your days complaining and less days actually do anything. Maybe you are depressed. Maybe a meeting could help?

Paula Albin

You are angry. I point that out to you. You get angrier. The children are now staying in their rooms because you complain about them constantly or are yelling at me. What's wrong now? I quit attending the meetings like you have asked me to. I even cut back on my many hours of volunteer service. I am home any time that I am not working. My best friend Connie moved to the city leaving me without a close friend to talk to. I guess misery loves company and you demand my company while you are clean and miserable. I also read somewhere that many Heroin addicts have rage issues. Maybe that is why you are always screaming? You tell me to stop reading so many damn books!

Any friends I did have found reasons to no longer visit. I guess I really don't need a social life. It's just you and me. The children spend all their time locked in their rooms. When we do gather at the kitchen table everyone watches when you enter the room. We watch how you set the cup down. If you slam the cup; we all leave. Invisible eggshells scattered on the floors. No matter how much we clean, how much we love, how much we avoid contact with you, we all walk on them eggshells when you are home.

Addicted to an Addict

You get angry over nothing lately. You have gotten so angry once you actually punched the refrigerator and broke you hand. Maybe you were just paying that refrigerator back for breaking your arm? This just doesn't make sense. You are punching walls and appliances and I am afraid of what's next?

Your yelling has gotten worse. It is almost daily now. The children are looking forward to going with their dad to get away from the fighting. What are we fighting about this time? Someone left a cup on the table. Someone left their shoes in the living room. Someone didn't fill the ice trays again. These are tiny things that just don't matter.

What does matter is that $20.00 missing from my change jar. It's my birthday and I wanted to buy that fountain for my garden. You asked me for $60.00 and I was short. I went to raid the jar just to find the money missing. I confronted you about it. You said the kids must have taken it. The kids are never home alone to get to the bedroom to steal from me. They want for nothing and have never stolen from me. You have a history of stealing from me. You pried my wedding ring right off the wall. You never admitted to that either but I never forgot.

Paula Albin

You were the Federal Hill Bandit at one time and made a career at stealing.

I have to tell you and I know you will be angry but your incessant ranting and raging has got to stop. I need the truth about the missing money. Instead of the truth and an apology you hand me $20.00 to replace it. We need a break from your anger. I need the truth for once. You decide it best if you move down the street to stay will Billy for awhile. I watch you leave and this time I didn't cry.

You are just a block down the street but already the house seems to breathe a sigh of relief. The children come out of hiding. My friends still won't come into the house but at least I can have a phone conversation without you yelling in the background. And I see you every day. You stop by to do your laundry, take a hot shower or grab some food. You yell about something and leave again. You'll get through it. I bought you some Saint John's Wart to soothe your anger. That just made you madder still. I don't know what to do. Maybe the Heroin kept you calm? This can't be the real you; or is it?

Connie called to tell me she is coming up today from the

city. That's terrific! How I have missed her for so many months. We can get some Chinese food and talk about our lives. I have an earful to share with her about you. I know you don't like me going anywhere but she is my best friend and its only lunch after all. You and I can watch a movie when I get back. It's Friday and I have all weekend to spend with you.

You come over for books. You're bored and want to read manuals. I drop the bombshell. I couldn't even imagine what you would have done. I told you I was going to lunch with Connie. You lost your mind. Something snapped. I saw it in your eyes. You screamed at me that she was a fat whore and I wasn't allowed to go anywhere. Before I could think straight I responded how she is my friend and at least she treats me good. You just came at me. I went to the kitchen sink. I always seem to be in the kitchen when I am upset. I remember you told me once how you beat your ex-wife in the kitchen and how most domestics happen in the kitchen. I was afraid. For the first time ever I was afraid of you. You grabbed me by my neck and pushed my back against the sink. You were screaming in my face. You called me a whore. You said you should bash in my pretty face. I'll never forget that. Hot tears were just streaming down my cheeks. You said you would give me something to cry about. Just like my father used to say. You took your open hand and smacked me on the top of my head. You just looked at me for a second and let me go. You slammed your head down on the kitchen island and told me go ahead and bash your head in. I actually considered it for a moment but only shook my head no slowly. I was shocked. I was mortified. The love of my life threatened to hurt me. My daughter heard it. She started recording it on her cell phone. She came out and grabbed the house phone. She said she was calling the police. You told me to get that phone. You told me you would kill her, kill me, kill us if I didn't get that phone. I knocked on her door and told her to give it to me. I asked you to leave please. You demanded the house phone. I begged you not to take it knowing that is the only house phone I have. While still holding the phone you grabbed me by the back of my hair and demanded money. I went cold. I didn't even feel the pain anymore. I looked you in the eyes and said as slowly and plainly as I could that I gave you everything I have and I have nothing more to give. You let me go. You told me I was not to leave the house. You would be watching. You also said I better not call the cops. If you seen any cops you would come back. With that said, you turned and walked away.

That was one of the hardest decisions I ever made. My love- my life, he would never forgive me. I know it. I hesitated for what seemed like an eternity. Then I walked to the back yard and made the call. I asked the police to meet me at the station because he was watching my house. Then I cried and a part of me died inside.

I filed the report. It was hard seeing the police because of who I am in this small town. I have worked with these same men. I was now just a victim instead of a savior. I was no longer the super hero. I failed. They arrested him. Connie stopped by for lunch but that didn't happen. Instead of a girls afternoon out she took me to the court house to get an order of protection. She stayed with me the entire day and made sure I was safe and ok when we finally made it home. My best friend supported me through this loss; this tragedy. I will be forever thankful for her strength and wisdom.

Paula Albin

Cleaning Out The Closet

2011
BY: Paula Oliver

The old tattered sweater I've had for 25 years

It's kept me warm It's wiped away many tears...

It was given to me Long ago in my youth

From the boy who first kissed me His lies I believe truth...

I kept that sweater Waiting for his return

But sooner or later We all must learn...

Love shouldn't hurt Love doesn't make you cry

True love stays It doesn't say goodbye...

After all these years That man is still a boy.

Who played with my heart Like it was a toy...

So that old ugly sweater I'll wear no more

I won't be fooled Like I was before...

It's time to clean out my closet...

SICK TWIST OF FATE

I'm not actually sure how I got sick again? Maybe the stress of your addiction or the stress of my addiction to save you from yourself has caused my liver damage. Maybe it is that sick twist of fate finally coming back at me for all those times I made bad choices growing up. It could be as simple as being with you while you use a dirty needle. Either way, I got sick. I was working and crying and stressing so much after you were arrested. I borrowed a few handguns so I could sleep. I dreamed you broke into the house to kill me. I dreamed I killed you and then killed myself. How funny; just like our Pantera love song; "I kill myself for you- I kill you for myself".

It is Turkey time in my little town. I'm scheduled to sell raffle tickets for a local organization and also to help serve the annual Thanksgiving meal for the locals. I just need to finish work and head over to the meetings. I've been so very tired and stressed lately. Leaving work I run into a friend of mine. Our boys play together at school. I have known this cowboy for 15 years. He's going through a divorce and we're talking about setting up a play date for the kids. Then he notices something I haven't. My eyes are completely yellow. My skin is glowing orange. This is pretty scary. His son has a condition and so he sees this often. I have acute jaundice. He insists that I go to the nearest emergency room. I would have usually ignored any such advice but once I see how sick I was looking I did go with a friend.

The urgent care could not help me. They sent me to the hospital. I was pretty scared and feeling very alone. I called my ex-husband and he picked up the children from my house and kept them while the doctors admitted me. I was put through many tests and my blood was drawn two times a day. My liver was damaged so much they started talking to me about transplants. They asked me about any drug abuse or use of prescription drugs. They asked me about my drinking habits. I was insulted. Don't they know who I am? I've been clean for years! I just try to make everyone else around me as clean as I am. I walk a high road and drag everyone else on that road too. I am told if I don't do drugs than it could have been given to be by someone who does. Then I thought of you.

I stayed in the hospital for 10 days. Thanksgiving was

spent alone. I listened to music and slept most of the time. The doctors were as eager to release me as I was to go home. I didn't want to die there alone. I called Billy to tell him to let you know. The cowboy stopped in to check on me a few times. I wasn't completely alone. I had a few friends from work, Lion's Club and others stop by. Connie came over to see me too. With that Order of Protection in place you had an excuse not to contact me. Now you decide to be a law abiding citizen. How convenient it must be for you that you don't have to deal with me being sick or answer any questions about how I got this way.

When I get out of the hospital- I go to the court. You were there. Billy brought you. He's such a good friend to you and I am so happy you have him. It's so good to see you again. You are still so angry with me. It is all my fault you have to be in court. It is all my fault you couldn't contact me when I needed you. I try to remove the Protection Order but the judge does not agree. We finally agree to a modified Order so I can be there to help you but you cannot be in the house or around the children. That is the best I can do and it seems fair. Now I can see you again as much as I want and help you get better.

Dance with Death

BY: Paula Oliver
RE: suicide thoughts

Sweet death- my special friend,
Come dance with me once more.
Bring to me a simple end,
Finish what we started before…
No pills, no blade, no shotgun shell,
Just one quick embrace.
End for me this life of hell,
Draw me closer to thine face…
Oh, what hideous smile,
Icy, fleshless bone!
Stay for just a little while,
Don't leave me to live alone…
Take me in my sorrow,
To hold and to decay.
There will be no tomorrow,
It doesn't matter anyway…

ON THE MOVE

I don't know what exactly happened but you are moving again. You tell me it's all my fault that you have to move. When the police came over to arrest you for hurting me, the landlord wasn't happy and asked you to go. Billy still helps you and gives you work but you can't stay there anymore. Now you move only two blocks away to a trailer park. You are making payments on a beat up trailer and are slowly building it up to a suitable living condition. You ask me for deposit money and I gladly hand you over want you need. Now that the order is modified, I can see you and help you. I meet you at the store and buy you whatever you need. I am so happy you are only two blocks away and you are working hard to have something for yourself.

I visit you at the trailer. It does need a lot of work. No plumbing yet but you have most of what you need and are working full time now. You go to Don's trailer to shower everyday and this arrangement works for awhile. I see how hard you are working to start a life for yourself and am willing for help you in any way possible. You will do great! You will stay clean! You will be home again one day!

As much as I dream we will be together some day, I also am so very afraid of you. I can't help but watch the door and insist that you leave it open when I stop by. Talking with you frightens me as I may say something wrong and you attack me. I am so torn between my need to save you from yourself and save me from you.

You did apologize for grabbing me. I needed to hear that. You also said you were justified and that I asked for it. I didn't want to hear that. You tell me you are fighting me to keep me! That doesn't make sense. The visits are short but frequent. It seems you are putting weight on again and looking healthy. It also seems you need something almost daily from me. Your love is expensive. It has been costing me financially and emotionally. I pay the rent again for you and buy you more supplies. I spend as much time as I can with you while trying to continue to heal myself, work and maintain a household. I have friends again. The cowboy stops by and we talk about you. I cry to him about the situation and my feelings. My cowboy friend is afraid for my safety and my sanity. All the books say that domestic abuse escalates but I won't be a victim again. Never again.

Addicted to an Addict

Buried Treasure

2013
By; Paula Oliver

In red rock my stone heart you'll find
Where I leave my sorrow behind
Within you'll find my deepest secrets
Magic-laced letters and trinkets
Tokens, pictures and promises broken
3 letters full of words not spoken
In cedar box my treasure waits
Until I reach those pearly gates
My box is buried among the dead
Securely tucked in my child's bed
And as always once a year
I'll stop by and shed a tear
Of what was and what shall never be
For him- for you- for eternity…

R-E-S-P-E-C-T

I guess your latest place of employment did you wrong. It seems everyone does you wrong at some point and you retaliate. Your hours were cut which left you feeling disrespected. So you muscle a paycheck out of the owner and walk out. Way to make friends and play nice! Haven't you learned yet anything I have been trying to teach you? Small town, big mouths and nothing but drama. Now where are you going to get the money for your rent? I can't continue to pay your way.

It's always a question of respect to you. I disrespect you when I go out with friends. My children disrespect you when they leave their clothes on the bathroom floor. The dog disrespects you when he barks too loud. The neighbors disrespect you when you are yelling at me in the yard and they stop to look.

You get no respect. Of course it is a question of respect when something personal goes missing and is sold for dope. I feel disrespected when a man puts his hands on my throat and threatens to kill me. My friends feel a touch of disrespect when they are in my living room and you walk by yelling "*what the fuck are you looking at?*" Or you call them fat whores.

I'm sure Al feels disrespected when he asks you to pay the trailer payment you agreed to and your response is "*fuck off.*" I offered to pay it in full but you already made a promise and an arrangement. Al's son Lance doesn't disrespect you but has lost all respect *for* you. You just tell me Al lost an ally and probably the rest of the money owed on the trailer.

I don't know how Billy ever disrespected you? He was giving you so much work. I think he was afraid of you. Billy is a timid old man who works hard to live a simple life. He has a girlfriend and a mother who finances his business. He tells me that you and he are no longer working together. You have been bullying all of the money from all of the jobs and he can't go home with nothing. You take the money and he does the work. He is just trying to survive in this little town like the rest of us and you are too angry to work with, you are sloppy at best and you don't show up at the job sites on many occasions. I wouldn't use Billy as a reference if I were you. That was a sad day when he told me he could no longer help you and continue to be your friend. He was a great friend to you and I found comfort knowing that he was there to help when I couldn't be.

It must have been a complete disrespect to you when the judge ordered mandatory anger management classes. You said there is no way you would take any class the "*The Man*" orders you to take. You will do it when you want to. I also find it rather disrespectful to refer to the DA as a little girl. Maybe you have been "behind the bars" longer than she has been wearing those big-girl panties, but seriously it is rather disrespectful to say such things in court. Being in the jail system for so long must have had taken its toll on your way of thinking. Whenever someone talks to you and you don't agree with what they say, walk too close to you and maybe touch you or looks at you and you feel uncomfortable, then you feel disrespected. Everything is not always about you and you need to stop taking everything personally. This is not prison. We are all free to do what we want.

Respect is something earned and is not a given right. You reflect in others what you yourself are feeling, doing and giving to the universe. It saddens me to see you this way and hear you talk like this. You get no respect because you give no respect. I'm afraid I may not be able to save you after all these years of trying.

Leaving Me

2011
By: Paula Oliver

There is no such thing as forever it's all a flipping lie
Cause sooner or later All things must die
And as I close my eyes I'll lay here and cry
While you pack your things Without saying goodbye
I could fall to my knees Beg you to stay
But sooner or later You'd leave anyway
All things that I've loved They've been taken from me
My lover, my husband Even my baby
How foolish to think I could start over again
That somehow this lost love found Would have no end
You were no ripple In my perfect pond
So much worse More and beyond
A tidal wave of sorrow
Who sold me a tomorrow
That shall never be
A you and me for eternity…

RIDE OF THE CALVARY

My great friend the cowboy reminds me so much of myself. He is forever saving people. He's a young simple man going through a divorce of his own. I've known him for years. I have always thought him to be so respectful and handsome. Of course, as a loyal wife years ago I have never done anything dishonorable. My ex-husband used to tease me relentlessly about the young boy I was drooling over. That's the thing about a good marriage; you should be able to share anything and everything with your partner. My ex-husband and I were great friends and still are, he just couldn't stop sleeping around. That's his addiction and I am not the person to fix that anymore.

Who would have thought a cowboy and a city girl would be friends? What could we possibly have in common to talk about: Children, community, addiction? Mr. Cowboy is going through a divorce. He was married the same day Wesley and I planned to be married. His estranged wife has anger issues and he has on more than one occasion felt her wrath. Wesley gets pretty angry too and likes to abuse me.

Addicted to an Addict

Old friends find comfort and someone who understands. The universe is so kind and it really helps to have someone to talk to. So our boys play together and we just talk. It's nice and easy and healing. I think he's cute and he thinks I'm cute too. He says to me "life is like a biscuit... sometimes you get honey and sometimes you don't". Well I prefer gravy but still it's a great message. It's good to have friends without the pressure of a title, a hat to wear or a mask to hide behind. My cowboy friend doesn't need saving. He just needs time to heal. And I don't need saving but my own time to heal. Maybe one day he'll ask me to dance. Maybe one day he'll teach this old city girl the Texas Two Step or better yet how to Waltz. I don't think I will wear that gray sweater to any more dances.

Paula Albin

The Hero

2011

By; Paula Oliver

I will save the world but who will save me?
From my darkness, my pain, my misery
I heal your wounds and steal your pain
I bring you sunshine when there is rain
I keep you safe I lift you high
And when you're better you'll say goodbye
I am one to admire
For one who aspires
To change this ugly place
To be more than a pretty face
But there's a price for perfect
Which may change your perception
Of how you think of me
And what you really want to be
Behind these eyes are tears
Lonely have been my years
My smile is just a mask

I wear to tackle the task
Of answering the hero's call
To give you all- my all
But when the day is done
I watch the setting sun
I'll wonder why it had to be
There is nothing left for me
I give you all my energy
Leaving my soul empty
When you're safe and warm at home
Here I'll sit all alone
To be a hero is overrated
It leaves me feeling cold and jaded
So don't save the world,
don't be like me
Save yourself and just be happy…

TRIALS AND TRIBULATIONS

It is a busy two weeks for me. Thank goodness I have some vacation time left. My mom flew out to show some support and accompany me to court. You have taken this whole domestic issue to trial. Why don't you just say you are sorry and take the classes? It's so easy just to play nice. Why must you do everything the hard way?

I am not just going to court. I also have a follow-up doctor appointment as well. They are concerned about some tumor markers or something and I have to deal with that too. I'm so tired of dying. I just want to live a little more, dance some and write.

I don't talk to you anymore. Since the last visit I told you I had a friend to talk to about my feelings for you and you snapped. You didn't hit me but you were visibly shaking and very angry. You called me a whore. I wasn't doing anything wrong! I came to you and explained that we were only friends and that I need a friend who understands. You threatened to kill me if you ever heard I was dating him. I don't date. I never dated. I was always married or with you.

You have friends. Your friend Don up the street lets you use his shower. I found out he is also an active Heroin addict. You swear you are helping him to get clean. You also have Kristin hanging around all the time. She is known to be a meth addict who gave away her children so she could continue using free of the burden of motherhood.

Then there is dirty Val. Val has been telling people around town that you two are "*an item*". These are not my kind of people. They never really were. With all these lovely people visiting you why is it I am still paying your rent? This is the last month you live off of me. I've learned a new word: **NO**.

The doctor says I'm going to live. My liver is completely healed. The tumor markers are small and there is no need for concern at the moment. I don't believe them. I am scheduled for a recheck on my birthday. I've come to accept that we all die. Most of us don't have a say in how it will happen. But in the end we all get to the same place. Today I choose to live again while I still have time to do so.

Court was completely uneventful. You didn't even have the nerve to show up. They still made me go through the

Addicted to an Addict

whole story again and again about what happened. I am so sick of reliving that moment. How much I want it to go away and how much I wish it never happened. You text me before court and tell me if I just lie then it would go away. If I tell them I was mistaken then you would be ok. You would come home and never do it again. You said you didn't want me look bad or have to call me a liar. Oh how much that shows you never really knew me. I always do the right thing even if it hurts. This hurt so much. To tell the public exactly what happened and how helpless I was to stop it. To admit to myself and the world that I was a co-dependent enabler who needed your love and acceptance. I had to admit I was an addict. I was addicted to you.

Since you didn't show up for court there was a failure-to-appear warrant along with a sentencing. That's what you wanted. You didn't want classes so I guess it is off to jail. Maybe you can do classes on the inside? You call me after court to tell me it's all my fault. Your life is my fault. How I killed you by loving you and how you hope I die alone and in pain. I told you I was no longer riding on your bi-polar express and that I was done feeling guilty. I gave you everything I had and I have nothing more to give. I wished you love and peace and told you to get help. You told me you were going to kill yourself and this is the first bag of dope you've had in two years. If I ever wanted to say goodbye I better hurry.

The usual pain runs through me. I cry. I go numb. This is old hat for me now. I can't fight the addiction. I have to go to you. I always have to go. I told you if you are on that needle again then you are already dead to me. That statement still ringing in my ears... Ok, just one more time and I won't see you again on this side of life. Just one more time.

I give in to the temptation to answer the cry for help. You always knew how to pull my strings and make me dance for you. Reluctantly, I drive over to your place. You are not even home! I go looking for you. Why do I always keep looking for you? When will I learn? I stop by the store and the lady takes me to the back room. She is crying. She said the police were there and so was the ambulance. They had taken you away to the emergency room. She said you were dying. She said you hadn't eaten in two weeks and looked half dead. I know that look. I've seen you wear it before. It's the look of the active addict. So begins the search for the long lost love.

I call the hospitals. I call the morgues. I call your mother on the east coast. I call the jails. I check the internet and call everywhere again. I go to your trailer and open the door. You must have left something for me to find. I found the needles. I found the pot and the pipes and the empty bags of heroin. The place is destroyed. I also find the ramblings of a sick man in a journal written to me, for me and about me. I find the little trinkets you had made for me. I find your wallet and ID. I take your jacket, wallet and every piece of paper with my name on it. I also take the journal. Some light reading before bed.

The landlord stops by while I am rummaging through the place. She knows me well. She sees me every month paying your rent. She informs me that you have been evicted and have three days to move since you assaulted Don down the street. It was a fight over something missing. Maybe that is where all those baggies came from? I told her what happened. I told her you were rushed to the hospital due to an overdose. She wasn't surprised. She said Dirty Val wants to get into the trailer to get her spoons. The spoons they cook the dope with I wonder? I inform the landlord that one no is welcome to enter the trailer until I take whatever I wanted. I requested that everyone allow me to pack in peace and solitude. I had to say goodbye...again.

The second day into my search for you the police stopped by my house. They can't find you either. I was dumbfounded. They are the police after all. They had you. How can they just lose you? I called the hospital several more times. I was desperate. I finally found one nurse who would talk to me. I said I had your wallet and that I was the closest thing you had in this state to family. She said she remembered you and that you wouldn't need your wallet. She said you were not going to *"make it."* I froze. My blood ran cold and my face went pale. I refused to faint again. I had to stay calm and call your mother. I left your mother the contact information and didn't call her again for a few weeks.

In the meantime, it seemed you were more popular than you realized. All the "not my kind of people" were driving by the house. Even a few stopped and asked where you were. I told them all, anyone that would listen, that you were dead. I was stopped on the streets while going to the store. I was called at work and contacted on my cell phone. Every dirty addict in town wanted to know what happened. Except Val… she did not approach me. She knew better. I made it very clear that no one was welcome to my gate and no one was allowed to talk to my children. I told the children that you moved away forever.

After a month I have cleaned the house of everything you left. I contacted your mother. I packed the little bit of things I was able to get out of that death box of a trailer. I finished writing in your journal. I even packed that ugly gray sweater. Everything is ready to go back east to your mom. The junk pile is gone now. Even the refrigerator was donated. The neighborhood is quiet again. No more ripples in my pond. I have buried your needles, wind chime, letters and your pictures at my son's grave. I have a tattoo on each leg of the loves I have buried. One in memory of my son and one of a fallen angel for you. Today I have more angels than friends and I am ok with that. After all these years I am finally ready. I am putting you down like a bad habit. I am kicking my addiction.

Paula Albin

She is ME
By: Paula Oliver

She is kind she is wise,
she has gray in her hair.
She has sad brown eyes,
she has a story to share.
Of love lost, love found,
love lost again.
But here the story doesn't end.
She is good she is strong
She believed that love had prevailed
here she was wrong
Her hero had fallen- he failed
He left her heart broke
He took all her money
To him it was a joke.
To her- not so funny.
But today she's found
Love that will last
Not in the future
Not from the past
She took a look in the mirror
Smiled at what she saw
Someone to be proud of
Someone who stands tall
She is……..ME

Writers Cramp Publishing

www.ingramcontent.com/pod-product-compliance
Lightning Source LLC
Chambersburg PA
CBHW081355040426
42451CB00017B/3464